Within Darkness & Light
A Collection of Poetry

Compiled & Edited By

pAul B mOrris

nOthing BOOKS

Published in Great Britain in 2017 by Paul B Morris, Nothing Books Publishing, West Midlands, UK

ISBN:
ISBN-13: 978-1975631307
ISBN-10: 1975631307

Content

Foreword

Welcome one and all to **Within Darkness & Light**, a collection of poetry inspired by the dark and light of human emotions.

As you venture forward through these pages, you will have the pleasure of experiencing 133 excellent emotive poems, written by many talented poets, who have all donated their work in aid of charity. I hope you are moved by this collection.

To those readers who have purchased this book, I thank you for that. In doing so, you have contributed to raising money towards a leading UK mental health charity that is incredibly close to my heart and mind. One that does so much to support souls and families who live with mental health issues. I am personally grateful for the past support I've received from this major mental health charity as are a number of the fellow contributors.

Thank you

Paul B Morris

Transylvanian Dawn
By Al Barz

The lightest hour is just before dusk,
vicious sunshine searing the eyes
like pus in a frying pan, crackling destruction,
undermining dark cloud's throes
with brightest golden-yellow edge,
until its death knell slams shut the day.

Now in the gloaming, creatures stir
their furry bodies, flex their talons,
move stealthily into the darkening air
that beckons them to survive at night
as they could never in fiendish day,
with tiny echo sounds of flight.

Here is existence's finest hour.
Lifting the lid on my arousal,
I climb from dead day's shrouded box,
stretch the centuries from my bones,
lick the dust from my two long canines
seeking the warmth of your fresh blood.

To a Child on a Summer Bedtime
By Al Barz

You do not want to go to bed, and nor do I.
Days so full of comfort, safety, peace and love
Are to be held with hands and head and heart,
extended
As long as daylight lingers in the evening sky.

But there will be another time in future's grasp
When fears and tears are banished from the
memory
Not to return when the night has cast its net
And gathered shoals of daylight from the evening
sky.

Those crumbling thoughts of panic, dread and
emptiness
Have to be scattered on the rippling river waters
So sweet sleep slumbers, free of jangling pains,
May thickly spread from daylight's pot of evening
skies.

So don your nightwear, clothe your mind in happy
day
Cleanse your mouth of best-forgotten yester-tastes
You do not want to go to bed and nor do I
But we are blessed with joys of days and daylight
lingering in the evening sky.

Am I OK?
By Alan Glover

Am I OK?
I think so
Sometimes
Maybe
Sometimes not
Depends on what
The fragile balance of chemical circumstances
That tips the scales one way
Then for no reason the other
Do I need help?
I think so
Sometimes
Maybe
Sometimes not
Depends on what
What kind of help

Who/What/When/Why
Do I know the reason why?
Sometimes
Maybe
Sometimes not.

One Day In May
By Alan Glover

I open the curtains & stare at the day
Look at the sky and suss out the weather
Reflect on the forecast from 12 hours ago
It's wrong again, as usual

Check again & all seems normal
But something catches my eye
Flitting and swooping against the clouds
And I realise in an instant

This is no normal day
The swifts are back for summer
And the day just got a whole lot better.

Being a Superhero isn't an Illness
By Alan Wilkinson

Manic depression, the disease of clowns,
Smiling outwardly when feeling incredibly down.
Depressive phases when death seems near,
Manic times when you live without fear.

The moments of normality are by far the worse,
How the rest of you tolerate normality; surely it's a
curse?
Tablets work for a while but the power of the mind
wins,
Chemicals are far too predictable for a body that
constantly spins.

Call it what you will but I don't think bipolar means
ill,
After all being a superhero from time to time is a
skill,
Just leave me alone when I'm fighting the evil
within,
That's the only time superhero me isn't functioning.

Central Character
By Allan lake

In front of Uluru or Big Ben,

at the entrance of Disneyland,

the Grand Ole Opry, Graceland,

atop Balinese elephant, Great Wall

of China, strolling through a garden

in Kyoto, a murder camp in Poland.

Same face with minor alterations:

happy face, sad, cheeky, deep in thought

as she studies a tourist menu in Verona.

Her impressed "friends" have Liked,

Loved and Laughed. Happy faces,

wow faces, tearful boohoo faces.

Some even commented, Lucky You!

You rock girl! Please forward some

warm weather back here asap, LoL.

Did you meet your Romeo in Verona?

That comment remained unLiked.

Leading lady in role of her adventurous

life, since the death of that childless aunt,

the one with all those investments

that were promptly rolled into travel

fund for her solitary, deserving self.

No more teaching, no more books,

no more students' distracted looks.

She didn't meet a Romeo anywhere

along the way but did decide to buy

a designer cat when she returns

home and name it just that.

Potential for further Facebook

fulfillment has occurred to her.

Happy Face
By Amanda Glover

The down
is flat black like the coffee,
but without cream.
It cannot be sweetened
and is served with a guilty question mark.

The up
is where I am, mostly.
It tastes like the glacier cherries
I used to swipe out of my gran's pantry.
I got caught but it was worth it.

I didn't let sticky hands bother me then
and most things still don't.
More guilt to be kept a lid on,
just like I should've done with those cherries.
The truth will out.

My Ode to Death
By Andrew Lennon

I've seen deaths face and I told him no.
As I've done many times before.
I'll leave here when I choose to go.
I turn my back and close the door.
As serpent fingers grab my feet.
And try to pull me underground.
I fight my way out from defeat.
And stop to take a look around.
Lights gaze at me from up high.
And I see hope now through the trees.
I'm soaring through the painted sky.
And hear birds singing in the breeze.
I'll climb these stairs and won't look down.
Strength in my legs has now returned.
Stand on deaths head and bend his crown.
His face is gone, his shadow's burned.
I march on now, head high and say.
With freedom rushing through my veins.
"I'll greet you death, but not today."
Until then only hope remains.

These Days
By Angie Payne

Shit, Snot, Puss, Piss
Is our Society
No one cares these days
It`s a selfish mentality.

Politicians
Paedophiles
There is no longer peace
In these Western Isles.

John is hooked on methadone
All kids want
Is a new mobile phone.

Homeless people sit and stare
They can't believe
That we don't care.

Everyone is getting in debt
So, they can buy
A new TV Set.

Look after your own
And stranger danger
Leads to more isolation
And mental failure.

Hammer it down
On this bloody table
I wanna leave this world
It's too unstable.

Bones and Patience
By Austin Muratori

The skeleton of pain bares the weight
of my tortured soul.
Fear is the glue that holds together
my vacantly warped sanity.

Together the bones work in unison to
Support my infected patience.
All an effort to survive the malignancy
of a tattered life.

Faintest Dose
By Austin Muratori

Wandering through the valley of the lost
I feel the emptiness grow.
The expanse of torment is a process consumed with
pain.

An illness with a cure so inconceivable
that it no longer exists in reality.

Progress is slow as I venture on into the dark abyss.
Only the faintest dose of light would be treatment
enough.
For I could leave this dreadful place.

Though my body is dying, my drive is strong.
I aim to find that light,
whatever the cost.

Always and Forever
By Becky Narron

How do I tell you
And make you understand
I love you forever
It's just who I am

I will walk beside you
Holding your hand
Proud to be yours
And that you are my man

I want to tell the world
Just how special you are
You are just what I wished for
On that shooting star

Together through anything
Love will abound
Because I love you
You amazing man

Just love me and hold me
Close to your heart
Whispering words
To my soul doesn't depart

My heart feels like
it will explode from my chest
But that is just love baby
To me you are the best

I don't have enough words
To tell you my dear
As long as you are with me
I will have no more fear.

Lost
By Becky Narron

Lost in the ocean
Deep under the sea
Can't find my way back
someone please save me

No one is around
And Nobody cares
I try to scream
But there's nobody there

I swallow water
It's salty brine
Someone please hurry
There isn't much time

The lower I sink
The worst I feel
Being alone is the
worst of all deals.

Pillbox
By Benjamin Blake

Side effects
Of a misplaced mind
The walls are warping
Before skitterish eyes
Can't stop shaking
Can't shake the feeling
That something's about to go
Completely and utterly wrong.

No Knives
By Benjamin Blake

A rare euphoric day
The old knife in the gut
Still and quiet
For the first time
In a long time

Dappled autumn light
Dancing across the pages
Of a book of poetry penned
By a man buried
On a slight hill
Somewhere in Los Angeles

The cat wasn't really dead
Which is always a nice relief
And the dog is sunning himself
In an empty room

A man may even
Believe in love
In these all-too-elusive moments.

Wrists Full of Tears
By Bruce Lockhart 2nd

She's found throughout life,
through her every struggle, every strife,
 That religion is darkness and hers lay at the end of
a knife.
Religion, doesn't change…the gravestone where
she'll lie
Yet in this moment, she sees clearly, Jesus cry—
His wounds always open, always there, always
nigh.
Crimson tears, streak her own bleeding wrists,
Her agony and anguish, indeed do exist.
Since childhood her world was *always* more;
more feeling, more depth, more pain—her reward.
His tears now spilling heavily into the waters of her
bath;
she bleeds, oh she bleeds, spent tears finding their
path.
Tracing barren canyons on a pristine, angelic
face—
What horror her true love shall find her in this
place.
Flashes, of a life half lived, swirling, filling her
mind.
Is it really so hard, for humanity, to offer
compassion?
 To find a way to be kind.
Pills lie scattered, a cursed message on the floor
that this poison, a newfound lobotomy for the
despaired, for the poor.

She knows, if her soul was a color it would be a deep, swirling blue.

How much pain can one person take? She prays her death will leave a clue.

To be lost so completely, that this *sin* be your only choice.

Why, you ask?

Isn't it funny at the end…now they yearn to hear your fading voice.

The time draws near, she can finally let go.

Yet a moment of clarity, in the one verse she knows.

Aye, though I walk through the valley of the shadow of death,

I shall fear no evil, for thou art with me…

He was always with us. Her breaking heart tries to plead.

Your love…

He'll never recover,

Not for the rest of his life.

Can't you see,

he'll bleed, you're just passing on the knife?

A door opens from beneath her watery, red grave.

He's always running late, but if grace is his love,

then maybe, just maybe, her life he could save.

This beautiful soul at the end of her rope.

Her pain entirely compounded—

to lose life within you, something so unfounded.

She'd lost a child, plunging into pure misery.

Her world fell apart, made her sink so far adrift.

The man of her dreams rushing to her, to close more than one rift.

Towels from shaking hands wrap around her limp
wrists;
searching his mind while he calls, begging for
an ambulance.
Where did he go wrong, where was his love amiss?
On a dark, rainy night, they saw Jesus Christ,
 crying over her skin.
Was it all over, would Death take her and win?
Yet she awoke, to machines beeping, and lover's
hand in her palm,
a thought rooted itself inside her like a forgotten
Psalm.
Maybe loving him, and he loving her…
could be that very slice of Heaven
she'd been searching for.

The Diary Entry Before Your Suicide Note
By Casey Bailey

Dear Diary,

I tried to do it today, I couldn't.
I will do it tomorrow, I have to.

If I don't stand up for me,
nobody will, and even if I do, they won't,
I can't wait for a hero to save me,
I've got to save myself.
I feel like it's now or never,
and I never want to feel like now again.

I can't hear about the difference
between sticks and stones, and words again,
When physical pain is the only distraction
that I have from the real hurt that I feel.

I will do it tomorrow, I have to,
and the next time I write in this book,
it won't be to say he's done it again.
If he does, I probably won't feel like writing.

I Know How I'm Supposed to Feel
By Casey Bailey

I know how I'm supposed to feel.
I know the ground doesn't swallow people,
I know that walls don't move to close in on me.
Walls don't move.
Collars on t-shirts don't tighten.
I know this.
But this isn't all I know.

I have sat on the bottom of the ocean,
I have drowned with the weight of the sea on top of me.
I have opened my eyes to find an exam hall.

Bright sun doesn't brighten dark days.
Wise words can't calm troubled waters,
troubled waters of a beating heart,
that shake and break minds that were once steady.

I know how I'm supposed to feel.
I know I've never had surgery on my chest.
So why have I felt hands creeping inside my rib cage?
Why have I felt fists,
squeezing my lungs, thumping my heart,
blocking my throat so I can't breathe,
can't speak, can't scream for help!
And I need help!

I know how I'm supposed to feel,
I know, I know, I know. But I don't feel like that.

Grasp
By Charlotte Postings

We have a bond, you and I
A connection like no other
We're incredibly close and I know you'll always be
there for me
I count on you to be there on every bad day, and
even every good
You sit and wait for me to crave
You wait for me to need you
I always, always need you
You're my only escape
My only release of pain
You make me feel alive
You make me feel like I can leave all the suffering
behind
You give me hope
You give me all the wrong reasons to live
I have you to fall back on
You're not really there for me
You need me to need you
You give me satisfaction, yet at the same time cause
more damage than good
You're never good
You're manipulative and mean
All I need is to feel that drag across my skin, the
blood pouring down like rain
You're my biggest enemy and I don't know how to
ever escape your grasp
I just need comfort, but you gave me an addiction.

There is Nothing
By Cherry Doyle

There is nothing
in the woods, no silken breeze

nothing to crack
the black bulk of trees

nothing but breath
to muddy the diamond night

nothing under our feet
but spent moonlight

nothing but you, me,
a dog and a distant car

there is nothing
between us and the stars.

Parked Up
By Cherry Doyle

Out where the fox's bark
separates vertebrae
as easily as its teeth

the mouse's eyes swallow
the glacial bead of the moon,

pupal tears squirm
at their corners.

Urgent grey
fogs the windscreen;

unseen predation
burdens the night.

The utter darkness
gets under my skin;

even as I turn the key,
a chill dew settles in my veins.

Not Right
By Clive Oseman

 I know... I should be happy,
and I am.
But I'm not.
Well, I dunno, you know?

It makes no sense to you?
You think it does to me?

Everything's good, but it's not right.

Yes, They're real tears...

It's true I've lots of friends.
and earn decent money.
So, what do I do, pretend?
Say there's not a part of me
spoiling to tear it all apart,
bring me crashing down
to where I was before
to take me right back to the start?

I don't KNOW why!
Maybe I don't deserve what I've got.
Of COURSE I can't allow it to.
What do you suggest for the best?
I put these feelings in a box
and burn them?

Don't you think I would if I could?
that I hate this silent torture,

the void I feel but can't locate?

I know you're trying to be a mate,
but it doesn't help. Not at this minute.
Come back when it's finished,
when I can appreciate it all again
and I'll apologise.

But now I'll hide my eyes
behind dark glasses if I must
until the moment passes.
I don't know when.
It's just.........

Crowds
By Clive Oseman

It took what seemed an eternity
but steadily the crowds I craved
began to show
passing through turnstiles
from isolation to inclusion,
starting with a trickle
till they clicked at double speed
to feed the need I held.

The days are gone when all stood still
and I counted all the open spaces
wishing they were faces,
gateways to a meeting of minds
once either side of wide divides.
How many more? I don't keep score.
It's my desire, like an open door
with all life's colours to explore.

There's plentiful supply.
If I stretched them all from end to end
they would make a pathway long enough
to pretend the dark days never happened.

Well did they, anyway?
Who can say what was real
through all that time spent hoping,
knowing I wasn't coping, but never breaking free?

Was it really me at all?
Could it be the game is won?

The crowds are noisy,
it's not easy to pick up on particulars,
especially today.
Are they coming or going away?
I ask because all I hear is fear
and I sense the light may disappear.

8 Balls and Cheese Blintzes
By Cole Bauer

Marco liked travel
Marco liked buying and selling narcotics
Marco liked food
Marco liked getting high
Marco liked booze
Marco liked men

Marco had his family and friends
Marco had stories
Marco had scams
Marco had money
Marco had all he ever liked and wanted

Now
According to most
Marco has God
Because with that man
He can make any sin
Sound delicious
A loss for Satan

Steam from the Theme
By Cole Bauer

Life
Has a way
Of throwing themes
Into your life constantly
Whether you realize it
Or not

From homes
To schools and work
Moving back and forth
To the same places
The repetitive routine
The redundant struggle

It is all about
What you fill
Your life with
Mine is always hellish
And I try so hard
For change and improvement
To make it heavenly

Maybe you're better off
Maybe you don't notice
I am envious
I hate themes!
I hate the shit jobs!
I hate the road trips!
I hate being behind on it all!
Hate! Hate! Hate! Hate!

As the Sun Sets
By D13

The sun is warm on the nape of my neck,
Just as your hand was when we met.

But as the sun sets, the warmth dwindles,
Just like your hand as you slowly drift away.

The sun has set and darkness looms.
All I have left are these thoughts of you.

With time, I was left questioning;
Which parts were true?

Too much time I've had to think,
Too much time for thoughts to become other
things…

Another Day Passes
By D13

Another day passes.
Another night draws in.

I miss you more than I ever realised.
Things are happening. Things are changing.

Yet...

I often find myself wishing,
I could tell you all about them.

Dark Children
By Dan Oram

The Dark children
Their faces pale, upturned
Hearts so fragile
Their clothes - Lace, leather, velvet
Blacks - Purples - Reds -
Together they look like wounds
Make up - Made up -
Lips like red gashes
Pouring out their fears, smashing their hearts
Raging, calling, Arms raised as if to pull
Angels from their places and pour their darkness
Into them
Mouths like poison - cruel, seductive
Eyes like stars - hungry for something unattainable
They   court   fear – Even Death – like   moths drawn
to a flame
The Dark Children
The Dark, pretty, children
Who loves you?

Don't Try This at Home
By Dan Oram

Take the blade,
Watch it for a while,
One has to summon up the courage to do this,
Do this properly.
Find the Spot, pick it carefully.
Stretch the skin beneath the fingers,
Apply the knife.
Again.
Again.
Again.
It's funny, but they never seem,
Sharp enough.
It takes a lot of effort to make the,
Blood come.
Over the next few days,
Worry the wound,
Pull it apart and run your fingernail,
Across it.
Eventually, you'll get the *scar*.
Another scar, Another tally, Another reminder,
That you're still…
…Alive

Fire Escape
By Em Dehaney

Come, walk the fire with me
Just for today.
Slowly,
Deliberately,
Footstep by footstep
Bare skin on burning coal.
Salamander,
I cut off a limb
A new clutch of nerves exposed;
Raw, electric.
Lightening trees
Spread their boughs.
Needles and pins and knives and saw blades
And razor edged sharks teeth
Piercing through muscle and bone.
Leg in a bear trap,
Arm in a sling,
Fingers are tingling,
Pain fibres sing.
I only have so many spoons,
I sleep under tramadol moons.
When walking and sitting
And talking
Is exhausting.
I do not get better,
I do not get well.
No remission, no respite,
No release from this Hell.
Proceed calmly to the fire exit,
There is only one way out.

Of what they call
The Suicide Disease.

Morning on Ice
By Femi Abidogun

It is pitch dark.
But even in the boundless thickness
of this impeccable darkness
I can still
see the light.
For you make this dreary night
dazzle and gleam
so bright
such that
all of a sudden,
I'm in no hurry
to meet
sunrise.

A Locksmith Called Mel
By Gabriella K A Gay

Lost somewhere,
and all my prayers to St.Anthony returned
unopened.
Mummy didn't have the key,
or the names of saints to talk to me about this.
So I sat in the hall,
on the cold Minton floor.
I lay
flat on my back to breathe deeply.
With cheek on tile I looked to my right.
They walk the same way.
Stepped over me in their heels, with their babies,
husbands and holiday tans.
They chose life.
Simple.
Plan.
Follow an age-old path.
to fall in love,
into marriage, into parenthood, a job, a house, a
car,
into death.
To my left was an emergency escape.
It seemed closer.
But it took a locksmith called Mel and the love of
two friends
To stop me choosing it.

I used to own nothing,
so I was proud of the bunch of keys collected.

They showed what I'd achieved through
determination.
But now they were lost,
somewhere,
so high above my head I couldn't reach them.
Trapped in a hall painted white.
A prisoner in the life
I lay
flat on my back to breathe deeply.
Lay just awake,
contemplating the doors in this hall
that locked me out
and locked me in here
and Mum didn't have the key.
St.Anthony didn't answer,
And I didn't have other saints to talk to about this.
To my left was an emergency escape.
But thankfully the keys were closer.
when two friends and a locksmith called Mel,
who knew the heart of each and every lock
helped
elevate me enough to
walk.
Reach my keys,
And pick the master one,
To hang above my bed
Unlock boxed dreams,
And finding the value of what lay inside.

Spring
By Gabriella K A Gay

Every day begins and ends in darkness.
Some days die too young.
Mine did.
I wept them away,
again,
then phoned my son to say,
Don't buy me flowers,
bring me a garden.
Bring me Earth Glaze and Indian Ivy hope.
Promise.

I used to be that person
who'd frown at the price of a Scarlet Wonder
shrub
and moan that dibblets were far too dear.
But now I see the value of gardens-
The care, commitment and faith
it takes.
A covenant with seed,
to give it what it needs.
It takes
nutrients, water, light, the right soil
and a belief in many tomorrows.
It gives.
So bring me a bulb, I say.
I'll plant it in auburn falls,
Let it turn my thoughts to spring.
Bring me a young cherry tree, I say.
I'll plant it today so deep in soil,

and take shade in its prunus pink perfection of
tomorrow.
Promise.

When I'm old don't buy a zimmer,
bring me a mower
to back and forth
slow in lines of green.
I'll back and forth.
minding human nature.
I will
stop worrying about the future,
dwelling on the past
and smell the grass still here in this present.
Promise.

I don't won't want shop bought flowers,
I told him.
Stalks cut short
in a home,
to wither and wilt in careless hands.
Invest in a nursery, I say.
Bring me children.
Promise.
We'll dig deep in muck,
Spread sunflower seeds to heal,
Glow
And cleanse the soil.
Cleanse the souls of those stuck.
Those searching for a little place of peace,
Waiting for light when the day resurrects
And a better garden every year.

Wood Spirits
By Gerald Kells

Inside a wood the Devil sits
and all around his minions flit -
it is not dark enough to see
their shadows move in silent fee

to one who offers wind and rain
and leaves that turn back down again.

When You Come to the End of Sleep
By Gerald Kells

When you come to the end of sleep
there is only waking up
and what you find in the world is never
the thing you lay down imagining.

The Sun Doesn't Shine Here Anymore
By Grace Dore

The sun doesn't shine here anymore
We live in darkness
You take over
Wrapping us in
Your cloak of anguish
And mistrust
Posing questions
With unattainable answers
Questions that didn't need to be asked
Rattling confusion
In our minds
Hurt pins us to the ground
Words are brandished
Mindless actions that
Have meaning - but no healing
Only darkness and gloom.
As I walk into the daylight
Darkness walks with me
Covering me so that I cannot see
Anything but the darkness within me
I see no hope, no light,
Just a sea of black waters
A sky of black vaporous clouds
Sunshine CANNOT & WILL NOT shine here
anymore.

Dawn
By Grace Dore

I roll over,
Into a foetal position
Seeking solace
But finding none
Pulling the duvet
Around me, lifelessly,
What is the point....
What am I here for....
What do I do
To contribute to this world...
I can't sleep,
I am so tired,
But think of nothing
But negative thoughts
Grey light penetrates
Through wooden blinds
I hear the first birds.
And even though
I hear sweet birdsong
I still feel unworthy
To be even here
I am all alone
Completely....
Wrapped in my own
Sad, droning thoughts
When will I feel better,
No relying on self - pity
No more denial
I have to face up
To this world, otherwise

I'm going down.
As the light gets stronger
Objects take shape
Becoming more familiar
My eyelids get heavier
My heartbeat is slow
I shut my eyes at last
And I know that maybe...
Just maybe, there is hope.

Mood Food
By Heidi Miller

A tense conversation I'm left feeling stressed
I was really just trying to do my best
Not sure how to process the resulting low mood
My brain cries out' Eat some food!'

Nothing healthy, salad won't do
We need sugary, fatty and salty too!
A Hob nob or three, dairy milk and a flake.
Searching the cupboard for the last Jaffa cake.

Whooo that all went in a bit too quick
Inevitably I now feel a little sick
The sugar high is wearing off
Here comes the crash, it can be rough.

The voice has gone quiet, for now at least
Satisfied by the secret feast
I am left feeling flat and fat and questioning why
next time I'm bored or depressed and defeated
This cycle will once again be repeated.

Blue Bus
By Ian Davies

Nights are worse
Slow, simmering slumbers
Where vagrant thoughts
Push out like blind sperm
In search of ova

Nights are worse
Where sixty watt suns
Obliterate horizons
And bathe dreams
In cancerous yellow light

Nights are worse
Bleak, bottomless graves for hope
Where roots of despair
Worm through
To disembowel the promise of deliverance

Nights are worse.

New Day
By Ian Davies

Nymphs dance on daydreams
Gliding spryly on sunbeams
To ease away winter borne ills

Dust babies minuet
Dazzling and teasing
My waking senses

Which drink in
Warm soothing draughts
The promise of coming release

From this chilled crypt
Of long harsh nights
And dreams of Daedalus

Flying higher
On waxen wings and string
To savour and soar

To the sun
My long lost queen
My guardian sister

Woodland Pond
By Ian Henery

Dragonflies skim the surface of the pond,
A portrait of calm in the woodland glade;
Mother moorhen calls and her chicks respond,
A visiting blackbird sings in the shade.
A bucolic scene no painter would shun,
Rows of bluebells dance in the evening sun.

Fox cubs gamble beneath towering fronds,
Verdant green, the colour of forest jade;
A sylvan retreat, out of time beyond -
Great god Pan, to whom the wild folk have prayed.
He plays his panpipes, summer has begun,
Rows of bluebells dance in the evening sun

Vengeful Ghosts
By Ian Henery

Memories haunt and shriek like vengeful ghosts
Rising up from tombs of eternal sleep;
They had been laid to rest and buried deep
Out of public sight and Heavenly Host.
My crime my ego, nothing left to boast;
A bitter harvest, have sown so shall reap.

There is so much of which I am ashamed
All on display in a heart of regret.
I fall to my knees and pray there`s hope yet
In repentance for all the sin and blamer.
True love and forgiveness, greater than fame,
Experienced before my life`s sun set.

Don't
By Ivan Zoric

Don't assume you know me,
what you see is but a ghost,
an apparition of life observed.
Flesh of it buried elsewhere.

Don't assume you know my story,
for my lies and my truths
Often share the same womb
Conjoined in waiting.

Don't assume you know my pain,
although it's written across my face.
The transgression is mine alone
a metaphor you'll never get.

Don't assume you know my smile,
For it is a shadow puppet
The hands that move it
Scratch my back bloody

Don't assume you know my reason
When I am gone.
Logic is fool's gold of this world
lulling us into false certainty.

Don't assume you know me.

I never even knew myself.

A Battle with Myself
By J. L. Lane

Nobody said that living was easy,
But no one ever said it would be this hard.
Nobody said I'd sail through life,
But no one told me it'd leave me scarred.

Everyone told me I was stronger than this,
But no one had a real cure.
Everybody said I could fight my demons,
But nobody ever sounded sure.

I wrote my feelings down in a letter,
And then I tore that letter up.
I popped the pills into my mouth,
And then drank the water from the cup.

My father was the one who found me,
Empty pill sleeves all around me.
He called the ambulance when he saw my wrists,
Still bleeding and in agony.

The doctors told me I needed counselling,
And I knew that they were right.
But what could they really do for me?
They couldn't be there day and night.

The choice was mine in the end,
It was up to me to fight.
But I would not be strong enough yet,
It took me six more years to see the light.

The world told me to grow up,
Before I was truly ready.
Life told me to mature,
Before my emotions were ever steady.

It's been seven years now,
But I still bare my many scars.
Although they've faded to silver,
They are my restraints; my silver bars.

They show my battle with my demons.
They are the marks of a tiresome war.
I punished myself time and again,
Until my soul just couldn't take anymore.

Hurting myself didn't make anything better,
It didn't solve a single thing.
All it did was numb me for a while,
And prolong my suffering.

Self-harm was like an addiction for me,
One I knew I had to kick.
It was a never-ending wall I had to demolish,
And I did it brick by brick.

There is no immediate fix I can tell you of.
There's no cure upon the shelf.
All anyone can do is take some time,
And learn to love yourself.

Your Own Worst Enemy
By J. L. Lane

What do you do when your mind is your enemy?
When these feelings and emotions drain all of your
energy?
When the sanctuary inside your mind becomes a
dark place to be,
When the light fades and you can no longer see?
A place you fear most in the world that was once
your safe haven,
Now suddenly a place you've somehow become a
slave in.
You keep busy, trying to tell yourself it's okay,
But no matter how much you try, the voices won't
go away.
They fill you full of hatred, self-doubt and fear,
From a place that was once so bright and clear,
Now taken from you, ripped away at the core.
Leaving you with an empty void you just can't fill
anymore.
As a child you're told never to talk to strangers,
But who's left when you are a foreigner in your
own mind and surrounded by dangers?
You feel like you are coming apart at the hinges,
But you still try to hold on tight.
You feel like the whole world looks at you and
cringes,
Like you're the monster in the night.
You are crippled by your own brain, crippled by
depression.
Your worst enemy becomes your own reflection.

The insults you whisper to yourself become louder,
until almost deafening.
You beat yourself up until finally it becomes life
threatening.
All the noise inside of yourself, you wish you could
silence.
All of the commotion, animosity and all the
violence.
But stop for a moment and listen,
Take the key and free me from this prison.
I'm here to tell you to stay strong,
You may have forgotten me but I've been here all
along.
I won't hurt you, come nearer.
Come and face me in the mirror.
I'm the one who suffered your suppression,
The one you ignored over the depression.
I'm the voice that told you you're beautiful, clever,
unique,
Not hated or alone or useless or weak.
I'm the one who loved you all these years,
The one who saw you for you and wanted to keep
you near.
I'm the one who kept your head above water,
I never left you to the slaughter.
It's time to rise up above the negativity.
I'm here for you now and for all eternity.
I'm the truth in this crazy maze of lies.
I'm the one who feels the pain of your cries,
Who fights their way through the battlefield of your
mind,
To make it to you and tell you to be kind,
Be kind to yourself even in the darkest of times.

I am you and you are mine.
I will shelter you from the pain,
From all of the other voices in your brain.
So, what do you do when your mind is your worst
enemy?
I'll tell you what you do, you just think of me.

Love
By James Josiah

Love,
one word,
four letters.
An emotion.
A quickened heartbeat.
A breath caught in your throat.
A chemical reaction.
If only it was that simple.
Love is all of that but so much more.
A way back for the lost, a second chance.
A rubber ring for the drowning man.
A welcoming light in the dark.
A smile after a hard day.
A breath caught in your throat.
A quickened heartbeat.
An emotion.
Four letters.
One word.
Love.

Coping Mechanism
By James Josiah

Paint the smile on your face
Tell your reflection everything is going to be
alright
Bury the demons
Pantomime normality
Carry on the best you can because you promised
yourself you wouldn't think about the other options
anymore,
Hide the razors
And the pills
Ignore the voice in the back of your head
Everything may not be ok
But you're alive
And some days that's enough.

The Man at the Top of the Stair
By James Michael Shoberg

Not one soul believes us, and nor do they care,
They say, "There's no Man at the Top of the Stair."
But Marc and I've seen him, and felt the vile glare,
That's cast by the Man at the Top of the Stair.
His presence is known by the chill in the air,
As shadows congeal at the top of the stair.
We quake in our beds, each repeating this prayer:
"Protect us, O Lord, from the Man on the Stair."
But still he returns, and we brothers must bear
That figure who floats at the top of the stair.
So, through the long nights we await morning's
flare,
To drive off the Man at the Top of the Stair.
Does he then withdraw to some sinister lair?
A fitting retreat for the Man on the Stair.
I whispered tonight as he passed, "Marc, look
there!
He's taken his place at the top of the stair!"
My brother replied, "Michael! Oh! Should I dare?
To run to the bathroom, I must cross the stair.
But I cannot hold it! I'll burst soon, I swear!
I fear I must face him, the Man on the Stair."
I tried to dissuade Marc: "We're safe as a pair—
Please stay here with me and away from the stair.
That grim apparition would surely ensnare
A foolish young boy who would dash toward the
stair—"
But heedless, he sprang with a pluck that was rare.
And off Marc had darted, no doubt, toward the
stair.

The screaming came next, blending dread with despair.
"Mike, help me! He's horrid, the Man on the Stair!
His eyes burn like embers! His fingertips tear!
He's dragging me down through the dark of the stair!"
But I sat unmoving, refusing to share
My poor sibling's fate, which he met on the stair.
Then fluttering in came a small, ragged square—
A note, quite concise, from the Man on the Stair:

Dear Michael,
Your twin made for succulent fare.
I'll be back for seconds.
- The Man on the Stair

Now Donna's Gonna Wanna Breathe
By James Michael Shoberg

Now Donna's gonna wanna breathe as slowly as she
can.
"Stay calm. Try not to panic," shouts the elevator
man.
"I'll have ya free in half-a-jiff. Don't move," calls
out the voice.
And Donna, claustrophobic, gasped, "I hardly have
a choice!
It's not as if I'm free to roam down bright and
lengthy halls.
I'm in a small oppressive cube, with suffocating
walls!"
"Oh, this is just a hiccup," the repairman reassures,
"A rather common problem with these worn-out
metal doors,
And my ol' gal's seen better days. She's due to be
replaced."
 "Please don't antagonize her!" Donna counters him
with haste.
The old technician chuckles, "Yes, I heartily agree!
She's known to be quite peevish. There now! OPEN
SESAME!"
With timbre like a chalkboard, all four doors
screech gaping wide,
And there, beyond, a man invites the girl to step
outside.
The weathered soul in overalls persuades her with a
grin,
Encouraging the nervous child still shuddering
within.

"Now Donna's gonna wanna breathe," she thinks,
"Go on. You can,"
As she starts moving forward toward the elevator
man.
She peeks out through the portal and inhales a
greedy gulp,
Just as the elevator falls and turns her neck to pulp.
Cacophonous collision echoes upward through the
shaft.
And on the floor from which it plunged, a robe stirs
from the draft.
The codger, now a hooded skull, checks Donna off
his list,
"This job would get so boring if I didn't add a
twist.".

A Few Steps from the Road
By Jan Wilkins

I breathe the smell of moistened green
Twisting, tangled undergrowth neath
Dripping canopy of shadow- light; as
Foxgloves pierce through, spear like
On single stems of royal bells, deep
With nectar for searching bees.

 A Chiff Chaff greets me repeatedly
Calling of its identity; a Robin trills
Voices of cyclists filter then disappear
As I pause on the soft absorbing path
Self-Seeking in this woodland; who am I?
With lake side edge; a whisper away.

The Sea; my Cauldron
By Jan Hedger

Out of turbulent blackness
surges forth molten steel
spewing out its anger
upon the darkened shore.

The midnight sea is raging
 fuelled by a gale force wind
rain it is a lashing down
depression; it descends.

At each nautical mile of depth;
as space is a light year away;
light cannot penetrate, the
pervading, deepening darkness.

It is only blackness, that is
reflected; as a solid curtain
forever closed and locked in
perpetuity; in deep waters.

The Lucky One
By Janet Jenkins

If I hadn't cracked my mirror
that morning as I tripped over
your discarded towel.
If there'd been two-for-joy
magpies in the garden
instead of one-for-sorrow.

If I'd walked around
the builder's ladder,
caught autumn leaves
before they touched the floor,
met a black cat and found
a four-leaf clover.

If I'd pinned a horseshoe
above the door,
closed my umbrella
when I got inside
and put my new shoes
under the table…..

It wouldn't have made
a jot of difference;
you would have still left
the note
and our home,
to make *her* the lucky one.

Meditation
By Janet Jenkins

Meditation led me to a white deserted beach
and an aqua marine sea, where a porpoise floated
far out with me for many miles, until he left
and I dived down, down, into a dark place
where my senses were non-existent for minutes,
hours, or was it a decade? I have no idea how long.

When I re-emerged the sea had become surreal;
I was surrounded by comical beauty:
Sea horses blowing bubbles and chuckling,
turtles wearing tutus and waving wands,
gold sea urchins warbling in unison;
rainbow trout high jumping over starry shells.

Bells of different sizes started ringing, louder
and louder, until a school of dolphins shouted
"Stop!"
followed by a burst of whistles and clicks.
I was back in the room listening to a soft voice,
soothing music and the sound of my breathing ..
in...and out, as reality returned and recall began.

When the Voices Sleep
By Jason N Smith

Head full of talk thoughts hazy,
paranoia manifests and I think I'm going crazy.
closing my eyes conversing and no one's there,
my mind's an over-used bungee ready to tear.
I try and get a grip and grab hold of normality,
but the voices inside are equating insanity,
whispering words rather left alone,
causing me to scream like twenty
MEGAPHONES!
and I stop, and see all eyes on me,
because of let loose talk betraying too loudly,
with words so profound they drown me,
but at times can king and crown me.
Sometimes exasperating talk makes a skewed kind
of sense,
become engaging amazing like rap star 50 cents.
so, when traps are set and dangers roll,
It happens just like their script told unfolds.
No holds barred when the voices speak,
profanities no sane being repeats,
from these uninvited guests there from young,
now when silent it's like something's wrong.
Syllables sounding a susurrating background,
like a TV's on always the sound.
Is there a hex from birth that binds me?
Cause there is no escape from what's inside me
I try getting close so not alone from others,
but pain with disillusion my soul discovers.
My friends disappear so I shed a tear,
believing danger is near I tremble in fear.

then contemplation of death seems a viable and
achievable release,
because even in my prayers I can no longer find
peace.
RIP when the voices sleep.

Bipolar
By Jason N Smith

The mental tolls of moods extreme with apposing poles no in-betweens,
one-minute smiles the next a tear or filled with bile or vexed or fear.
In sadness soaked saturating pores or in happiness chocked as spirit soars
or grim atmosphere dark even in sun and raging inside at wrongs one has done
hyper energetic and so full of talk, then become a sick cipher with no energy to walk
hallucinations and stress and strains on the mind and paranoid delusions and the pain we find
Trapped in a life of surreal dreams in the mental tolls of moods extreme.

Involuntary Images
By Jean Aked

There is a dark and lonely place,
Cold and bleak like huge expanses of ice
That seem to go on forever.

Desolate is how it feels
To be tied to thoughts that never cease—
Thoughts that envelope and suffocate.

She Died For Love
By Jean Aked

She died for love only to find
He was no longer there;
There was no comfort in a tomb
That her love did not share.
Her cries like wails resounded
And yet no one could hear;
There was silence in the graveyard—
Continued through the years.

They made a pact to live in death
Together for all time;
Success could never mean regret,
His failure not a crime.
Once that step is taken
It can never be reversed,
No peace found in death—
A living hell on earth.

Out on the Park Bench
By Junk Talk Poet

The park benches are filling up,
With what the papers call the flops
And those dealt unfortunate hands.

They each and every one of them
The same, the same in their own way.
A mirrors' image of the next one,
The one before,
And what we could all have once been…
Who we could still be.

But we wander on passed.
Perusing through the pages of
Crisp books, hot off the press
In pretty book stores spat out
Of Rowling novels.

We sit and eat at café tables,
Chicken shops and tea rooms,
Fearing the impending doom
Of possibility, as we skip again
To another month. Stretching
Out our money like butter
Upon way too much bread.

We drive ourselves insane in night clubs
And believe for a split second that
We're immersing ourselves in culture.
We drink petrol tasting fluids
And post photos of ourselves

Having the time of our lives for
The sake of status updates.

We stare at our screens day in
Day out, night after night absorbing information,
As sales teams become blanket narration.

But you claim not to see it.

We fear it, but are impulsively lured into it,
Compulsively locked down by it for fear
Of missing out. Missing something.
Sometimes just missing the point.

We believe the papers,
The big money media companies
Concocting stories in office blocks.
Beaten over the back by editors
As they struggle to drum out another
Two bob story, that swills like
Seawater in the mind.

The minds of you.
But you claim not to see it.

Why do you listen to these magicians?
Who can pull tales from empty hats,
While sweating into ill-fitting suits.

Clichéd slogans ring out from the disaffected.
The deranged mouths of peacocks
Steeped in insecurity,

As another boy strikes and halts
The production line,
With a face like a mine field.
He becomes the hero for the
Affected, he's unelected but revealed.

Even Oranges Reach Their 'Sell By' Date
By Junk Talk Poet

Seeing the world,
Exposing all its angles.
Like the segments of an orange
Rotting on its own axis.
The skin coming loose
In its basket.
Melting down to the gritty bit,
The pith, stringy sinews
Like spiders' webs,
Old, forgotten, barely breathing
And dead.
Dejected, surpassed projected
And dead.
Its population fuelled on dread
And bordering extinction.
Unable to function, becoming mere fiction,
Becoming the dead.

A Bird Flies West
By Kathryn Azarpay

Speeding over him a bird flies west,
skimming tips of turbulent peaks,
spray tingles on a still warm cheek,
something arcane is pricked.
Knuckles white loosen at the heavy groan,
a call to his dark fathomless swaddling,
to be untraceable in his vastness.
In briny air open eyed she catches the swelling
accepts his unyielding embrace
sweeping her deep through blue green streams
where shafts of light split and fade.
Frozen arms clutch and crush breathless,
from beneath tender ribs issue
her last sighs until tingling limbs are numbed,
and the thick silence of nothingness descends.
No more the siren calls,
and shamrock shores wait alone
for a bird who fell for a fickle love.

Bliss
By Kathryn Azarpay

I've got this fixation with paper.
I've got this fixation with pen and ink.
They beckon me to bear my soul.
They beckon me to spill my guts.
I'm compelled almost to death,
I'm compelled almost to life.
If I'm spilled on the pristine page,
If I'm spilled in black and white,
shall they cradle my words
and love them back?
Shall they cradle my soul
and rock it gently?
I fear paper will have no mercy.
I fear pen and ink will cut me down.
So, for another day I'll let them rest,
to remain admired from a distance safe.
But they whisper, 'come on face your fears.'
And with renewed determination,
I say watch this space.
You bring me close to the precipice
with your open invitation.
I jump this time without hesitation
into oblivion, in bliss.

Lighthouses
By Kerry Cooke

 Blades of light
slicing through the bleak
blind
Searching my skin for rise and fall
like a lighthouse
scanning the blackness
for rock and breath

My stomach is a fist
the tightness scaling
my lonely throat
My nails engrave my palms with shame
sore eyes, sighing, begging for the light

A salty tear cuts across my cheek
A trench of self-hate and pain
I will the white light
to reflect the red regret
and build a prism with all my colours

The white energy of dawn
flushes a sorrowful tide
and pushes weathered shells
along the beach
smooth and new

Slowly inhaling the healing rays
my chest expands like a parachute, full
with cold relief
First light invites me

to exhale hard
all the salt water and rock
and flood my lungs
with only oxygen and compassion

My Mother's words
are a lighthouse
"each day is a new dawn,
my love"
A sunrise of red
scars, healing and
hoping.

A Path Well Lit
By Kitty Kane

Once, when younger, I walked a path well lit,
Now, life worn, body broken, most of the light, well
it's a bit shit.
As children, we see this mortal coil with awe,
Now, as fully grown, I don't wish to be here
any more.

Not one moment, of this life I've known would I
change,
But the way this world is now, I hope the end is in
range.
They say we choose this life we are given, and how
we play it out,
But I'm not quite so sure of that, when I see those
who go without.

I've never been more certain than now, at the lack
of a higher power,
I've searched in every petal I see, in every shine of
sun, and each shower.
I walked along the path of light, I crawled along the
dark,
But every path I chose to follow, left upon me it's
mark.

I've many things, to be thankful for, so many things
I love,
Some folk I've met, have disgusted me, others fit
with me hand in glove.

The people I choose to care for, make my life rich
in a way,
But do I do the same for them? I ask myself each
day.

Doubt fills my mind when I ask of myself
this, every single day,
Although many try to change my thoughts, they
tend to stay this way.
Why, I ask, would anyone want the rather broken
me?
I'll one day soon, remove myself, and pray to
something, that happy without me my loved ones
will be.

A Flame That Never Dies
By Kitty Kane

A child was I, but a woman soon to be,
You walked into my life, my own heart stunned
me.
The most beautiful man I had ever seen,
But you on the arm of another made my eyes turn
green.

Time passed by, my heart still yearned,
Every day I waited, asked, listened and learned.
I entered your life with a hopeful heart,
Knowing not that the path you led me down would
be so dark.

Into your circle slowly I came,
So young, so raw, so innocent to play in your
game.
On bended knee you asked me, to take you for my
own,
Nothing that day would change my mind, all at once
I was fully grown.

Even today, I can't explain, how you made me feel
inside,
I cared not about your wrongs and folly, I wanted to
take this ride.
Your life was alien to mine in every single way,
But how I tried, I tried so hard to fit, in every single
way.

My dark path opened up for me, one day up in your
room,
The sweet smell of the joint you made swirled
around Like a perfume.
To me the drug you offered, I hesitated at first,
But then I drew the smoke deeply, and thought my
lungs would burst.

The giddy swirling of my mind was swift and
strong and true,
I didn't really like it much, but I needed to impress
you.
That day you took me by the hand and bade me
come with you,
And when I left the bedroom that day, I had become
someone new.

Never any regret have I felt, since giving you my
innocence,
But often I wonder, had I not been so young, would
my mind have shown more sense.
My love, my lust, my need, my urge, my primitive
desire,
You woke in me that fateful day, and my love
stoked it like a fire.

Your need to escape the confines of your
mind, grew always ever stronger,
The list of pills and potions you imbibed so much
grew steadily ever longer.
So strong was my need and my desire to keep you
by my side,

Everything else in my life I allowed, to begin
to slide.

The party life, we loved so much, it's toll began to
take,
My parents, brothers, sister, friends, with all I had
to fake.
So deep my love for you did run, it filled my soul
and heart,
Adept at hiding I became, deception became an art.

A love that burned so deep and true, with drugs was
thrice fold heightened,
To lose you, part of me, my whole, ever I was
frightened.
Like pinball balls, back and forth, together then
again apart,
I lost count my love, my soul mate true, of the times
you broke my heart.

Upon the line for you I placed, my life, my heart my
whole,
I think you never quite returned, the burning love
within my soul.
For you I would have walked ten years, and then I'd
walk ten more,
The only thing that would stop me love, would be
for me to die upon the floor.

The years passed on in tumultuous ways, our love a
strange affair,
You walked away, so many times, but to refuse
your return, I could not dare.

Always you, that turned from me, I could never turn away,
But you destroyed me more and more, with every passing day.

The highs we sought, the fun we'd had, was now so hard to achieve,
For you, so much you needed now, to make your normality leave.
Real life for you was never right, you needed to be high,
I knew something had to change, or we would surely die.

I cleaned myself at last I must, my body soul and mind,
But the strength I found to beat those drugs, in you we could not find.
The hardest thing, I ever did, was walk from you that night,
The one and only time I did, your world turned to eternal night.

I wasn't there, I did not see, what became of you my love,
I know you went to search for me, with your mind flying higher than a dove.
You climbed my house, three stories high, your shaking hands and feet did fumble,
And oh my love, my heart, my life, to the cold hard ground you did tumble.

One week you stayed, but did not wake, your life no longer your own,
Your broken body, killing you, through every single bone.
The time it came, to let you go, to let your soul fly free,
But every single day that's passed, oh how I wish It had been me.

No day goes by, no month, no year, that I do not think of you,
I've bargained, raged, offered up myself, but it seems I will, not do.
Your time was up, stolen from me, I never could again say,
How very much you meant to me, in every single way.

Sometimes, at night, I see you still, as if you had not left me,
But morning light, the breaking dawn, it takes you once again you see.
And now my love you are gone, and I can feel no more,
Like a helpless wave, lapping at the shore.

Our Intricate Demise
By Leanne Cooper

Crimson tides gush from a delicate tear,
washing over us like raging waters.
We are left drowning in their wake – a beautiful
intimacy spoiled with the roughness of our true
fate.
No more are we lovers, but still we use each other.
Selfishly we take from one another; connected in all
but a label.
What are we now?
Passionate in narcissism, we love to be wanted; to
be needed;
but then we leave each other behind, pretending that
this is the end.
Pride and jealousy trail claw marks down your back
as I stake claim to what will always be mine.
I fear that the scent of you on my skin, and the feel
of your lips upon my breasts will leave me ever
branded as your possession; a play thing to do with
as you will.
And though I hate to admit, I long for the feel of
your body pressed against mine;
to once again see the primal urgency in your eyes,
proving that, contrary to words, you do want this as
much as I.
Our intricate demise.

Noctivagant
By Leanne Cooper

I am the 2 AM mind fuck,
The questions unanswered.
I am the over thinking that keeps you awake;
The doubt which floods your soul.
I am the sickening panic attacks whilst you are
trying to sleep;
The blackness that clouds your thoughts.
I am the pain, deep down in your chest;
The sorrow and anguish which brings with it
unrest.
I am depression, I don't need an invite to stay;
I will settle down and get comfy
- I will not go away.

Absence and Wonder
By Lemmy Rushmore

What have I done
What will I do
I question this
While missing you

You're not here now
It's this I know
But what event
Brought you to go

What great mistake
Or tragedy
Might I have caused
To let this be

Am I just cursed
Or damaged wares
A long lost waste
Passed hopes and prayers

Must all I touch
Decay and rust
Must all I love
Just turn to dust…

Her
By Lemmy Rushmore

I can't picture a day
without you at my side
nor begin to explain
all these feelings I hide

you bring comfort and warmth
you bring light to my days
you're a goddess no less
one deserving my praise

you make me wanna be
you make me wanna try
till I think without out you
I might wither and die

you're exquisitely carved
you're divinely unique
till my heart skips a beat
if you do choose to speak

you're the hope that I lost
the tomorrows in store
you're the dream that came true
you're my whole world and more.

Lifeblood
By Linda Angel

They sent me off to Syria to document the war; I thought I'd have a painful job, too bloody to ignore. But once inside the outside of the coldest, newest hell, I found a limitation on the things that I would tell.

I didn't see what they did, like the rubble and the blood, or hear the screams of sorrow through the broken neighbourhood.

Behind bombed doors I didn't hear the terror they were dealt; in front of hell I stood with them, not feeling what they felt.

I didn't see or hear the dead, the dying, the bereaved; I didn't know their tears were red, for mine were so congealed.

I didn't see the children hidden under bricks of clay; I didn't know their names or where they'd liked to go to play.

I didn't feel the pain they felt; the struggle to survive. I didn't know the suffering of tiny little lives.

The things I saw in Syria were from another place; I looked upon the broken and I saw my daughter's face.

I held a crying mother as she mourned her children three; and all I thought right then and there was Thank Fuck It's Not Me.

From Syria I made a call with matters to report; my words were what I felt - not right to say the things I ought.

I spoke of how my children had enjoyed their Christmas Day, and how they'd been excited for the contents of a sleigh.

My kids were all so wonderful, I said with love and hope, not hearing any problem with the happy words I spoke.

I left the hell of Syria and took a flight right home, and as I flew I knew I'd have to cry into a poem.

The children there weren't Syrian, their blood belonged to me; the faces of the dying plucked straight from my family tree.

The falling bombs were merely seeds too late to be un-sown; and with the death of Syria, I looked and saw my own.

Sonnet 2,017
By Linda Angel

I'm grateful for the muses in my life:
The war and terror tearing Terra down~
For what else would my conscience have me write?
And what else to explore, or to expound?
Thank goodness for the blood and pain and death;
Without those things, no need for rhyming art.
We're lucky that we witness to such depths
The torture of our Earth's unbeaten heart.
How grateful we should be for politics;
How thankful for the fear of gods, and greed~
I pray that love and hope do not eclipse
The beauty of the war that poets need.
I lie: for song, I've lost my appetite;
I'd love to have no poetry to write.

Reclaiming the Knife
By Linda M. Crate

I only want peace in the sanctuary of my church.
So why must I wear the fabric of their doubts,
fears, and anger?
Why must the lacquer on my walls be of their
blood and tears?
My floors wet with their sweat and blood
their songs gnawing into bones,
and I want to ask why?
Why must I crucify myself for their comfort
to forget myself and my dreams
simply so they can live?
I took the knife that they stabbed in my back,
and carved their inheritance of hungry wolves and
then
climbed into my favourite tree to dine with the
ravens who had called foxes to open their
feast of blood moon flesh
upon the branches;
and I watched as I always watch
realizing that they did not even notice my going
because they found another to leech off of
perhaps her blood is more considerate and patient
that mine—
one day I know, she'll find me, and ask me:
sister why did I stay so long?

Seeking You no More
By Linda M. Crate

You shut me out of the light,
and into the darkness
meant for me to die beneath the snow;
but I came back
a stronger and more beautiful flower
than before shining with so much light that even
the
sun is blinded by my gaze—
your desires and lusts still consume you
without mercy like you who breaks hearts in the
same way,
and so you'll find I have no need of you even
if I still
care and love despite my knowledge
you're not worth anything I have to give;
just another ghost in the haunted house of my
darkest memories
without darkness there can be no light so I don't
sweat it
because one day I know this pain will end and you
will not be here
I will find peace and solace in the power and
strength of my dreams
won't lay where you left me in the snow
because I've already
burned away the architecture of your nightmares
to free myself from the darkest adventures
because I crave something better and less bitter than
discord.

Outside / Inside
By LM Cooke

We never understood,
Never shared our dreams or interests.
Never saw eye to eye -
But when you're gone there'll be fewer stories in
the world.

Outside children scream and rage against their lack
of meaning,
And teachers smash and steal while the parents of
the dead are keening.
Outside fires burn, shattered glass like jewels lies
gleaming.
Tales of strangers raped and robbed, outside, no one
hears their screaming.

And inside clocks tick on, and TVs shout the news
too loudly,
And pet hairs line the stairs while spiders build their
webs so proudly.
And inside teacakes toast, and tablets pile up in the
kitchen,
And all is calm and still – so still, you know there's
something missing.

Outside madness rules and Dionysus claims their
hearts.
Orpheus puts down his lute to let them all tear him
apart.
And inside nothing stirs, and Morpheus keeps all so
weary.

Heads nod on settees - a life once lived, now ending dreary.

We never understood,
Never shared our dreams or interests.
Never saw eye to eye -
But when you're gone there'll be fewer stories in the world here.

Rebirth
By Lynn White

I'm ready for the birth of a new day.
Ready for a pink dawn to rise
and break
full of possibilities,
as the light takes
over from the dark
and the day is born
again.
And I shall follow the road towards the light,
and leave the dark behind,
again.
But I have found that the dark always follows.
Catches up with me, as if it were the past.
If I hurry maybe I'll escape it this time.
Maybe I'll catch the light
and hold on to it and
not let it break
again.

One Day
By Lynn White

One day I'll see through the mist.
One day I'll find you again
and uncover what I let slip away
and become lost in the fog
and the forest.
One day I'll stop searching
and greet the mist with a smile
and watch it fade away
before it envelops me.
One day I'll greet the sun again
as the mist clears
one day at a time.

Nebulous Nightmare
By Mark Nye

'Separate the stars,
Defile their luminosity.
Lay in a sad state with the damned,
Even if they're madness to behold.

For glorious sinned atrocities,
A river of slaughter from the wounded slit.
Drove sweet blood to her parted lips,
To escape thine obsidian pit.

Defiled and deflowered,
Exiled from mind.
Her stone cold cunt,
Slavering delicious find.

Awakening, she climbed through dirt.
Her spirit soared past menstrual skies.
She outshone even the brightest star,
My leaden, dead virgin nebula.'

The Void
By Matt Humphries

The void between men is not healed from words
The loneliness we feel cannot be heard
The time that we spend in embrace with another
Is greater than speech in times of need

The soul closes in on winter nights
The warmth we feel is no mistake
In others company we grow and learn
Isolation is the human's great curse

The void we feel is far and wide
It spans the seas and mountains high
It harms our being and our bodies
Its cause's chaos and much worry

Words cannot heal bridge the void
Inside we die and just avoid
Therapy is the Holy Grail
To share is love and not self-denial.

It makes me sad,
To see humans.
Lost and lonely,
Caught in the revolving door.

It makes me realise,
We have to do more.
We have to listen and learn,
From the people in doorways.

Into the Collapses
By Matt Nunn

Not existing on the surface anymore
I am reduced to become a fading whispered echo
of who I presume to be.
Crumbled into the confused outskirts
of buried trauma freshly renewed
then fossilised as a crossed-out character in the
wrong story
who finds themselves as a fallen supernova
stumbling through empty passages
inside the swiftly re-arranging jumbled book of
days
whose words have become illiterate symbols
disembodied from their normal meanings,
and returned to bleak new depths as a liquidated
shadow frozen upon a memory of the sun with
somebody else's damaged head found being heavy
upon my shoulders,
like a previously undiscovered dying planet
infected by a conquering armada of creeping mental
aliens
all moodily crooning in hatefully grating jazz
voices,

"what a marvelous day for a nervous breakdown."

I am the Only One
By Matt Nunn

The day after I'd come back to sanctuary
feverishly feeling overcrowded
with anxious aliens
borrowing holes from the language
to chunter with in abusive fuel,

tilted by what I'd done and it had done to me
I bumped down the stair shaft in fractions
until landing in the isolating atmosphere
whispering in cold tongues
through the family parlour over-run
with the chipped blocks off themselves
that my favourite icebergs chose to expose.

Being too busy silently lingering out
freezing chastisement and getting angst-riddled
at regurgitated newspaper chunder they never
clocked
the hundred haunting shadows,
a dead worm choir impersonating soul singing
scratches
pouring from the uncomfortable pores'
underwiring my loose-fitting body.

Nor how special my unique strangeness was making
me.

Black Blood
By Matthew Cash

Forever must I crawl through the sodden fetid
faeces of this mortal coil?
The desire to lance this pus-filled rancid boil that
the happy call 'life'.
I want to end it in a flash of burning pain,
And from my wrists the ebb of blood shall drain.
To end this suffering, kept in this pit of melancholy
hopelessness
To cease this gangrenous putrid existence once and
for all.
Free myself from the things that I am,
The things that I do,
The things that I allow.
To sever my ties with this continuation,
My isolation,
Loneliness beyond restoration,
Hatred beyond redemption.
I want to dissolve the ties that bind me here,
Their coiled malevolence like barbed wire.
And feel ultimate release as all my life,
All my energy,
All my thought,
All my hurt,
All my depravation,
Surges out of my tortured, scarred unclean body.

Boo, Butterflies, Bukowski, Booze
By Mia Bauer

When time stands still and the progress is slow
We often dig deep to find the motivation to get us
started
The Lover and I traveled 10min up the street to sit
with an old friend.
This December day was the perfect setting for such
an occasion.
Rolling green hills in the distance, littered with lush
trees.
Beautifully well manicured grave stones in every
direction.
Two monarch butterflies paraded through the early
afternoon sky.
All of this was kissed by the golden glow of the sun
as we landed at the doorstep of our dear comrade.
Though it's not the first visit, each encounter feels
different.
We sat with Hank and enjoyed being in his
presence. The gifts left behind by previous guests.
We drank those gifts left behind by previous guests;
it's what the host wanted.
We laughed
We took photos
We shared this moment with friends
I watched the Lover recharge his momentum
His momentum recharged me
These visits always remind us
Of our purpose and path.

Untitled Emotion
By Mia Bauer

Another cliché:
Dirty motel room
Whiskey straight from the bottle
Weed in the hookah
Starving artist

The depression stage is set
So splendid in the early morning light

The thoughts are dark
A constant stream of negativity
Permeates and festers
Reminders of past failures
Feelings of restlessness
Creates a boiling rage

What was once an inner radiance
Has been eclipsed
By the depraved and desperate mindset
Emptiness fills the soul
And is seen in the eyes

Terrible thing to see
When the spark goes out
Yet even the Phoenix can rise from ash.

Isolation
By Michael Cronogue

They say no man is an island, yet for some this is
their daily reality;
Cast adrift from normality, they are like the rocky
outcrop in the ocean,
Always seen but rarely acknowledged.

The sense of loneliness pervades, ghosts of
memories past sometimes painful,
Entices a further withdrawal; reaching out becomes
harder, suffering in silence often
Preferable to letting outsiders try and reach in.

Who is this island, this rocky outcrop? Who is this
person who lives in such isolation,
Hidden from view, yet, still visible to us all?
Who is this person left alone to carry their invisible
burden, while life goes on all around?

This person can be anyone of us!

This person could be Me or You.

Sadness
By Matt Humphries

It makes me sad,
To see humans sit
Begging for change,
On litter strewn streets.

Sat in the cold,
Without a house or a home.
Cardboard boxes,
To shelter from cold.

It makes me sad,
We're at this point in time.
Where we are suspicious of need,
On our guard all the time.

Walking on past,
With our coffee in hand.
Second glance back,
As we wander inside.

It makes me sad,
To see problems galore.
To witness poverty,
On the steps of our door.

There's addicts in droves
Trying to score.
There's just no resources,
To care for them all.

Friday Morning 01:30
By Michael Cronogue

The desk light shines its beacon across the
top, where the PC lies open at a site called *The
Moth.* The china mug with horses rests on
a coaster, a treasured legacy from my late father.
Insomnia grips me like an ancient affliction, and
yet, it seems the best time for new creation.
The artistic mind fights its battles on so many
fronts, like armchair generals, always
willing to retreat or is
it advance? At Writers Circle last evening, we
plotted novels and opening
passages, prose to stimulate & excite, characters
fleshed out, plotlines made more concise.

A disposable fountain pen now sits in my
hand, symbol of short-term society at a glance,
the retractable pencil is banished to the pot, while
I try to least give this new
technology its chance. Essay, poem, sketch or short
story, which genre should I turn my mind to
tonight?
I turn on *iplayer* for some much
needed inspiration, seeking something a
little less topical in flavour. Politics is so
sterile today nobody trades real insults
anymore; "Debate" is
all about sound bites crafted solely for the 24hr
news, not sure for what they intend: to inform, or to
amuse?

Perhaps I will write a poem, a short concise
verse, a few musings on those loved ones
who have passed to their eternal rewards, while
those who are left, return to the grind
knowing they are still being watched
from heaven above. The screensaver appears, my
Grandson, Michael, resplendent in his *Ladies
Man* Sweater, now nine months old and already
trying to walk, memories of his father in years past,
a new generation to bear the family name, a lot to
live up to; God willing, he'll be equal to the task.

It is 03:30, and only the scratching of my pen can be
heard against the enveloping silence;
I sketch out ideas, checks lengths of verse and use
of iambic pentameters, even the creaking
of old floorboards cannot disturb my literary
thrall. They say the darkest hour is before the
dawn, but at least the moonless sky guards against
distractions. At last I feel the arrival of welcome
slumber, so I put down my pen and close the book.

Fortune indeed may favour the
brave, but only when you're lucid enough to
join in that number.

Love Addiction
By N. M. Meintjies

They have been warning me about all kind of
drugs.
But never have they warned me about the drug,
with beautiful eyes.
See, I'm so addicted to you,
that no psychologist
can get through the thought of your
fascination in my mind.

In the morning when I open my eyes,
another subject I can't find.
With the tickling feeling I felt when I fell for you,
somehow you managed to get into my body cells.
And every ounce of blood that runs through my
veins,
has a touch of you.
I believe on that day, that's when I lost myself
within you.

The thought of losing you ties stiff knots to my
soul.
It gets hard to breath,
I choke to the carbon monoxide of being without
you.
You happen to be my oxygen molecule.
You motivate to take yet another breath at life.
You are my life,
and I'll love and respect you as such.

Sleep
By Neil Richards

The light chatters to itself
It's never known darkness

Each hour we are cut from sleep
To check we are still breathing

The door to sleep must be left open.

The Wrong Tree
By Neil Richards

The wrong tree isn't barking
The chicken isn't sprung
The nest egg isn't hatching
The cat hasn't swung

The days aren't salad
The bell doesn't save
The wrist isn't slapped
The hands aren't safe

The mile isn't taken
The light wants to go out
Cats and dogs won't rain
Thomas will not doubt

The mirror will not look
Hand in hand has gone
The gas has been cooked
The race will not run

The candle will not hold
The tide is not turning
The fences cannot mend
The cloud has no lining.

Journey Before Dawn
By Neth Brown

Embracing denial, grabbing hands
Of those long distance runners
Reaching for batons.
enjoying the momentary down
Hill run. The very real
Doberman bark, chase, bite.
Breaking down in front of the inevitable
Punching the mirror
Finding the right door to walk out of.
Taking on a new perspective
Mapping out new ways
to dangerous places
Choosing a different cider, then
A different spirit (repeating)
Drinking to your reluctancy
of going home.
Putting off story telling
Walking a longer route home thinking
If you were slimmer...
Yearning for distraction, the
nightsong of owls or picking cat
Hairs off clothes, realising;
Millions of mayfly live in one day
And calf have more to look forward to.
Yours is a manic scramble
of back to back days.
Revisiting your ten-year-plan
Renewing all images
In your head start wishing on a risk
Tying loose ends.

Notes are piling and wires are fraying
Tarmac is becoming dust
The bony cloaked guy
Is wearing a bullet proof vest
You aim like a cock-eyed
Drunk at darts.
With vice in hand
Enjoy the dark
Before the dawn.

Working Class
By Neth Brown

Brown bottle necks are their bird
night-wear is their uniform
where every wish bone breaks even
urgencies of day and season
never seem to pass through here.

Hard water swans cladded wings
hake and sink with last year's dream
of revived factories and coal
of suit hugs from working fathers
no dates make these headlines
seagulls break morning: "nowhere to go"
there's more trash than meat on bones
empty hoods levelling the curb
all for one on this boomeranging road.

Milk is kept cold on windowsills
lager cans sing on broken steps
alley way wisdom and a bard's ink
stretches into a motionless blur
knock-off tat-shiners pray for copper
greasy blank-label odd-cuts lock jaws
ladies breaking leopard-seam unhinge them
little-look-away has not enough fingers
grandma-no-story latches ever tighter
unconventional vampires want youth
desires slurred on bus stops.

Wannabe mob-men, soon to be teen-dads
wannabe teachers, soon to be crazed moms

no role-models, think dole-figures
big-talkers beg with pigeons, no more
does the big spender bed with beauties
fishermen curse like desperate gypsies
'Pawn your sentiment' is todays sermon
newspapers are out, tattoos are in
charity bell-ringers are the dog's dinner
and so is tonight's and tomorrow's.

Those ever-enduring stone-squeezing
somehow living off the baron concrete
hope-hauling big-drinkers walking
doe-legged beneath the hammers
Currency cattle carrying this place.
Endurance Class.

The Darkest State of Mind
By Norbert Gora

From the source of lifetime
flowed the stream of the cursed past
a mixture of tears, pain and fear
poured into the form of depression.

With a mask of apparent happiness
stuck to the dull skin
I sobbed softly
amidst an anonymous set of faces.

An invisible tragedy of everyday
never ending battle
with fiends made of anxiety
you call it stupidity or lack of courage
but it was the darkest state of mind.

Something Else Instead
By Paul B Morris

I do not fear what I will become,
Though I am scared of walking blind.
Conflicted emotions wrestle daily,
Beating hard on my bruised mind.
It's way too easy to judge,
Those who surrender own life.
But not so easy to understand why,
So many reach for the knife.
Then they cut their arm,
Category self-harm,
No one's raised the alarm,
It's too late, they have calm!
But, where were you?
Discussing the needs,
Whilst the poor soul bleeds,
Yet another statistic is true.
It's a moment that I dread,
When another one is dead,
Punished by the voices in their head,
But everyone speaks of something else instead.

In My Arms
By Paul B Morris

I am whole when I am with you
for your light drowns out the darkness
forcing my static heart to beat loudly
I evolve in a love so true.

Pulling my soul free from the past
you engage me in the present
keeping a safe grip on my heart
presenting me with a love so eternal.

Forgive, that I wonder if I'm in a dream
for a love like this is surely fantasy
yet, I do know the answer to this line
as you are here, in my arms.

Saving my battered heart
you inject life into my veins
a drug so wildly addictive
I consume it wholeheartedly.

There is nothing more to consider
for all is presented to me in form
you are here and I know it is true
relishing this love so fine.

Sweet Angel from up above
know that my heart is truly yours
let me caress your sweet form
forevermore, holding you in my arms.

The Words I Love You
By Paul Bridgeman

The words I love you
Made my world spin a little easier,
Made my eyes brighter,
And my heart a little lighter,
Every day so very full,
Because the day it went away,
Everything became so grey,
Come back take it all away,
Was the mantra for each day,
When love has gone away,
Is there anything to say,
Until the grey is gone again,
For a few more clear days

The Grey Place
By Paul Bridgeman

I sit here in the grey place,
I sit here every day,
There is no noise here,
Everything has gone away,
I see the "real" world,
But it is transparent,
A filament a wraith,
Nothing really gets through,
I'll just wait here and recover,
It's the best thing I can do,
I see them all smile at me,
The ones who love me dear,
I just wish I had the strength to speak,
Say that for a while I will be here,
That it is not that I don't love you,
Or that I don't feel it returned,
Just my life has seen a fire,
I am still feeling it burn,
All I need is patience,
A little bit of care,
Tomorrow is a sunny day,
I'll be waiting for you there

Alone with the Quiet Day
By Peter Wilkes

Alone with the quiet day,
Alone, trying hard to pray
In solitude, and solemn thought
Tense, afraid and sorely fraught

Please to give me peace of mind
Sooth my thoughts this quiet time
Swathe my troubles all away
This silent, lonely, quiet day.

I feel a presence here with me
Comforting arm enfolding me
Soothing thoughts flood my mind
Loving feelings, peace I'll find.

Now I Have the strangest feeling
Just as if I have been sleeping
Peace and serenity comes to me
The pain and hurt has set me free.

A new day soon will dawn
Night will pass to another morn
The days ahead will be fine,
Thankful, for the quiet time.

Changing Times
By Peter Wilkes

I sit in the gardens
Adjoining our flats
Cursing the squirrels
And the old feral cats.

The birds are all roosting
And resting their song
The dark is descending,
The night will be long.

Cos the times they are a changing

I'm searching my mind
But I don't understand
What's wrong with the World,
What's wrong with the land.

What's wrong with the people
I just don't know.
Religion is struggling,
Which way should we go.

Cos the times they are a changing

I honoured my Father,
And I loved my Ma,
In seeking direction,
Do I follow a star?

And if I find one

Will it lead to the light?
Will I succeed with its gospel?
Or die in the fight.

Cos the times they are still changing.

Useless Flowers
By Phillip Binding

Annie used to paint.
Oh! How she slapped it on, the oil
the pastel, ink, pencil and chalk.
Annie was no saint,
she painted herself too, in soil.
and lies where dogs and lovers walk.

Jenny used to ride,
Oh, how she flew, hair burning bold,
wheels like tumbling planets of life.
But Jenny used to hide
when nightmares softly kissed her soul.
Her dreams were killed with twisting knife.

Heather used to run.
Oh, how her spikes struck sparks from grass!
legs all blurred like sepia prints.
But Heather lost the sun.
Life was a door she could not pass
though she made her escape long since.

We all used to know,
someone, someone like them all,
someone slowly inside dying.
We all did nothing
save maybe sit and watch them fall
and leave useless flowers lying.

Tides
By Phillip Binding

They couldn't find him but then
he couldn't find himself.
Only the sky seemed familiar
and the colour of sand.
He recognised the warm wind,
heard the rattle of pebbles,
saw bobbing lights far ahead -
enchanted, followed them.

They couldn't reach him, but then
he couldn't reach himself.
His heart set sail from his mind,
his soul swept out to sea.
Brought back at last to warm hearth
they looked hard in his eyes
but he couldn't see them anymore,
and he couldn't come home.

He sat on lonely chairs
but walking still inside,
following lights and horizons,
hearing the hum of waves.
Trapped in a landscape of flesh
his mind was pulled, in and out,
feeling the sun and moon call
through echoing ears, lost eyes.

They thought he'd slipped away but he
had slipped away from himself,
stolen by a beckoning tide,
a glittering sunlight, remembered beaches.

Lone
By Rebecca Lockwood

When I am alone
I wrap my own arms around my smaller waist
to feel
like someone is there.
Sometimes,
Most times
I am a part which is spare.

So I start digging with my fingernails
to get to my heart
and it is still
beating, each and all parts.

I am clawing at veins which are pulsing
and I imagine standing over my body
at my own wake.
Why did it come to this?
for reasons I must know,
with more worth than for God's sake.

Those days
the people I love regenerate into gargoyles
with carved dark eyes that lay
condescending down, crying soil
Onto me.

Unless you can tell me why
I refuse to let you in,
the door is locked, sealed and bolted
because those days I cannot settle to begin.

See the closer I get to the reason
the tougher the parasites teethe on my raped skin
as punishment for treason.

By Your Side
By Rebecca Lockwood

To have never seen the sun before
To go outside and have it sat neatly in your lap
For the seasons do time lapse
Years are seconds,
By your side.

To have intimacy outside of the bed
Within our fingertips pressing like
Forever lasting flowers when we hold hands
At God's feet equal,
By your side.

To have eternal trust as if
Granted at birth by the wise men
And the ability to sleep vulnerable and sound
As if I have never slept before
One together,
By your side.

To have happiness seeping out of
The tongue
Speaking true words
As if I have never spoke aloud before
For the poems do rhyme,
By your side.

To have the days stretch longer
And the nights seem so short
I cannot hear the ticking clocks
Behold I am safe with you

Reconcile me
Forever yours,
By your side.

Aspergers's Is Not A Curse – It Is Just a Difference
By Richard Allen Beevor

Asperger's Is Not A Curse - It Is Just A
Difference??????

Think!

You had it bad or worse,
here's the social outcast curse,
playing with toys, oops! no friends,
social awkwardness never ends,
keep your gaze fixed on one thing,
it may be enough, if not sing,
please don't look me in the eye,
I can't face you I'm just too shy,
that raging noise hurts my ear,
the feel of a touch brings me fear,
people speak, expect a reply,
I can't get started, they see not why,
suddenly I break the dam of silence,
but the words I use are extreme and bring violence,
putting out such wild logic in a whirl,
my odd speech scares every girl,
have to do things in exact routine,
must be just so to avoid dangers unseen,
hide away in my room of walls to talk to,
do they answer? of course they do!
try to walk without tripping,
always hit the ruts and on ice slipping,
try to speak but have no words,
have more in common with cats and birds,

gonna touch this door ten times,
it keeps at bay the nasty jibes.

See him he really is so weird.

Just a freak,
beat him up,
call him names,
make him cry.

Don't ask him,
he's no use,
push him out,
punch his face,
creepy jerk,
don't know nothing,
can't even talk! ! !

Asperger's is not a curse - it is just a difference

Maybe think before you accuse,
maybe stop before you abuse,
I'm in here trying to get out,
wanting to cry, even just shout,
perhaps I speak before I think,
it works that way it has no link,
tell me again how I'm so bad,
bad is bad but sad is sad.

THINK!

Beautiful Sound
By Richard Allen Beevor

 The distant sound of someone drilling,
the sound of life coming from the kitchen,
a cat that purrs its pleasure at rest,
gentle hum of the world at its best.

A tingle shivers through my brow,
simple sounds ignite and how
this sweet sensation invades my mind,
a pinnacle of bliss lets ties unbind.

How to describe this discordant sound,
that light's a beam in the pineal gland,
bring peace and serenity from around,
as this world sings from within its ground.

The singing waters flow soft a brook,
the turning rustle of page and book,
the simple sounds of life give way,
to the gates of heaven's bright new day.

Rid of You
By Richard Archer

I wanted to be rid
Of every trace of you.
I cleaned our flat
As if it was a crime scene,
The acrid smell of bleach
Erasing your scent.

Then I turn to myself
And the faded pattern on my arm
That spells out your name.
I want to ignore it
But I can feel movement and scratching
As if insect eggs
Were pulsating and hatching under my skin.

So I take my razor
And run it down my arm.
As the blue turns red
I peel your name away
Slice by bloody slice.
Until only a
Crimson gash remains.

I feed these slices to you
One by one.
An unholy communion.
Until you choke,
Screaming you still love me
But I know you're lying.

Light and Dark
By Richard Archer

I will never understand why some people love
light,
Personally I think it lacks discretion.
It loves to expose secrets
Shining its penetrating gaze
Straight into the dark corners of your life.
Revealing the pale white lines of old scars,
Showing nails chewed and bloody,
Tears forming in the corner of red eyes.
Faded blue worded on arms
That once spelled L.O.V.E.
When the light shines on you,
You're infamous for fifteen minutes.

Darkness I can appreciate.
It settles softly around you
Cloaking imperfections.
It is an equaliser,
Just because there's no light
Illumination needn't be lacking.
As when your vision's impaired
You can't judge until you've listened,
You can't form opinions until you stop and think.
Don't be afraid of darkness,
Just remember that when the light goes out
We can all become stars.

Well Hello World!
By Ricky L. Mohl Sr.

Well hello world! You're still here,
I lost my way thru the stratosphere.
Free flying on the whims of desire,
And a breeze of air lifts me higher.

Well hello world! Been quite a while,
And still I'm enamoured by the guile.
The beauty deception lies skin deep,
And above the soil rivers will weep.

Well hello world! Always the same,
Spin eternally in my window frame.
The mirror reflects the shadow play,
As a satin web will dance and sway.

Well hello world! Give us a greeting,
Time we have is quick and fleeting.
But still the weight is mine to hold,
And I cannot see past this blindfold.

Well hello world! Was nice to speak,
From ocean bottom to highest peak.
Blazing a circle in the dead of space,
Doing it always with care and grace.

Window Sill Dreams
By Ricky L. Mohl Sr.

I fell asleep on the window sill,
The evening sun upon me spill.
Off the river there came a mist,
Trailing fingers of gnarled twist.

I slipped under layer after layer,
Unheard words on silent prayer.
The rain dance on window pane,
Crystal streaks spread the stain.

I shiver in the abyss of dreams,
A dark hole filled with screams.
Such evil cries of black despair,
Sinister echoes in a nightmare.

I sleep so dead until the thunder
Tore me awake from the wonder.
Such release as I have never felt,
Escaping the fear that I was dealt.

I fell asleep on the window sill,
A crescent moon upon me spill.
Off the river there came a sound,
Where truth and lies can be found.

Love Gallery
By Rosemarie Gibson

I have become this way because of hurt
manufactured by torment,
turned into this canvas
that is nothing but a volcanic eruption
of misery, pain, fear and corruptive loathing
splashed into a gallery
full of other pretty faces -
Hang me on the noose that fits best into your
desired display
I have been battered by the revelation that feeling
hope or joy, and letting people in results in
the spears hurled at my back.
So ligature my wrists into the depths of you, for I
know no other way
and strip back my clothing, place me on a fashion
show
for my heart is there on the cuff
and it is the most beautiful thing I could wear
and also the most honest and true.

Her Love
By Rosemarie Gibson

I am cruel to her
this I know
it was the kindest care
that she did show

I feel I am a burden on her soft soul
but it is her encouragement
that makes me push to be whole

I have worn her down continuously
maybe I should walk away
if only to set her free from me

but that would be giving up
on proving that she is deserving of a kinder love
and that her care and belief is not wasted on me

so I will persevere on giving myself the love
that she has shown to me

She is the strongest person I know
she means more than I can ever show

so I will defend her in the battle of my own mind
and with this, my own strength, I will find

I have been cold to her
this I know
it is the ruthless of patience
that she'll always show

Big C
By Roylon Smith

I wanna tell you bout some body
That nobody wants to know
I wanna tell you bout some body
That nobody wants to know
I wanna tell you bout some body
That everybody knows

I'm talking bout Big C
Talking bout Big C
Talking bout Big C
I pray one day somebody eradicates you

He'll take your brother, your sister
Grand pa and grand ma, mother or father
He'll take your best friend too
He brings tears to our eyes
Pain to our hearts and devastation to our lives
It's in God's hands who survives

I'm talking bout Big C
Talking bout Big C
Talking bout Big C
I pray one day somebody eradicates you

Peace not Pieces
By Roylon Smith

People dying
Children crying
News reels are rolling
Bad news is comin

We want peace not pieces any more

Cold war is steaming
Soldiers are fighting
Intolerance rising
Violence is hap'ning

We want peace not pieces any more

Why can't we be like a jigsaw puzzle?
Joined together as one piece
Not scattered pieces of confusion
But united in peace not pieces

Neighbours disputing
Husbands abusing
Families fragmented
Disintegrated

We want peace not pieces any more

Airplanes are crashing
Cars are smashing
Vandals are wrecking
Lives are broken

Terrorists are maiming
Killing and hurting
Stabbing and bombing
Radicalising

We want peace not pieces any more

Voices in my Head
By Ryan Woods

You think that you know me,
but I can assure you that you don't.
You look into my eyes,
and think that you know what lies
Beyond…
But you are wrong.
I hide behind a locked door,
and I think that we will both agree
that the key
to set me free
is not in your possession…
Life has become a procession
of unfulfilled ambitions
and unrealised dreams.
The fabric of my very existence
is coming apart at the seams.
There is a darkness inside of me
that can block out the sun.
Lingering, like pestilence;
it is a loaded gun
with a hair trigger
and no safety catch.
It is a five-gallon drum of petroleum
and an inextinguishable match,
lying in wait
to create
an obverse reality
to the normality
that spews forth
from the smiles that mock me

from each framed photograph,
as I take this rusty razor blade
and carve your autograph
into my skin
and watch as your poison
bleeds to the surface
from within…
For a while the furnace
that fuels my anger,
settles down to a simmer,
but the glimmer
of hope
is short and bitter…
With a pitter,
and a patter,
each drop of blood
falls to the ground
like spent bullets
in a war of attrition.
It is a mission,
Impossible
to imagine a light
at the end of the tunnel.
So I funnel
all of my hatred
into this one moment in time…
If I'd had a dime
for every time that my emotions
caught in my gullet,
I could have fashioned them into a silver bullet
to release me from the pain,
put the muzzle to my forehead
and expand my brain,

Because
the voices in my head
tell me to do things that I find shocking.
There is no blocking
THEM∴
It is futile.
Images, so vile
that they burn black holes
into my soul
and torment me
Day and Night
are now my birth-right.
I can no longer tell
Wrong from Right…
Is the fight
even worth it anymore?
Or is it finally time to give in?
I grin…
and I bear it,
and wonder if I should share it.
But I never was the kind to share.
Besides, I wouldn't dare
unleash the Beast.
It would feast
on what little humanity I have left.
Bereft…
My life is a hurricane of emotions
that I struggle to control.
I am no role model.
I am no beauty queen.
Every second of my existence
is a scene
from a horror movie,

a blood splattered epic…
Jack be nimble,
Jack be quick,
Jack's gonna take this candlestick,
and burn this house to the ground…
I once was lost,
but now I'm found,
was blind,
but now I see.
There will be no saving grace
for me.
This was never going to be
A Fairy Tale,
nor have a Happy Ending.
My exit
Through The Gift Shop
is pending.
I've bought myself a one-way ticket
To Easy Street…
Every beat
of my heart,
every breath that I inhale,
threatens to de-rail
my journey
into Oblivion…
Life is given,
and life is taken away
in the blink of an eye.
I came,
I saw,
I stared into the maw
of my reflection…
Rejection

was a bitter pill to swallow.
I am hollow…
I am empty…
My heart has been wrought alveolate
by Grief.
Time…the Thief
Has erased things from my memory,
like an incendiary device.
So now, there is no more
Mr Nice Guy…
As hard as I may try,
I always fall short of the mark,
so
I forsook the Light,
and embraced the Dark.
Remember, if you can;
that once, I was a Mild Mannered Man…
But now, the three M's
have been replaced by the three R's…
Rage, Resentment, Regret…
I cannot forget,
and I cannot remember…
My life is little more than
an ember,
waiting to be extinguished…
Snuffed out, like a candle.
I can no longer handle
all that assaults my senses…
I built fences
around my feelings,
but each and every one of your
underhanded dealings
was like a coffin nail.

Your lies have grown stale,
like bread,
which you fed
to those who believed,
and perceived you as true.
So now, there is only one thing
left for me to do...
So, I will turn my back
and walk away.
After all,
tomorrow is another day...

Some Doors Should Never be Opened
By Ryan Woods

Some questions should never be asked.
Some thoughts should never be spoken.
Some doors should never be opened...
My soul has become a dark basement,
cold and damp
with walls that drip with regret.
My mind is a claustrophobic attic,
filled with cobwebs
and skeletons that hide in closets.
You shouldn't have come looking for me.
You should have left me with my demons.
I deserve them.
We are partners in crime,
Nickel and dime assassins,
Destroyers of dreams,
So it seems...
With a chisel
I whittle away
at my own self-worth,
giving birth
to Nothingness...
Did you think that kind words
could scale the walls that I have built around
myself?
Did you think that the warmth of your touch
could pierce my armour?
Perhaps you underestimated the depths
to which I have sunk.
Drowning in my moments of mediocrity,
I gasp for air no more.

I have resigned myself to my fate.
I realised too late
that it is futile
to expect anything more
from my fragmented existence.
Melancholy, is the symphony
that plays in my head, on repeat.
Lyrics that fall on deaf ears,
accompany a beat
that thumps like a failing heart,
as we embrace
in a Danse Macabre,
each playing our part
in this tragedy…
Surely you must see the light
fading from me…
Surely you must feel
the warmth ebbing away,
like a tide
that will never return to this shore…
I am grounded on a sandbank
of solitude
forevermore…
Enveloped by darkness,
I have but one match left.
Will it be *"Lucky Strike"*
or strike out?
I have no doubt
in my mind
that one day
you will find
the strength to go on.
"Carry on my wayward son.

There'll be peace when you are gone"
Those are the words
that should be left as an epitaph
to the aftermath
that I leave in my wake,
as I forsake
all that I hold dear…
It is as clear as mud
to you,
that I am no good
for you.
So take my advice
and take a hike.
I am the shrike
that will impale you
upon my crown of thorns.
It is our destiny
to be torn
asunder.
No wonder…
We are like chalk and cheese.
So please,
cease and desist
with your clandestine attempts
at reconciliation.
I have stated my declaration
of independence…
So gather up the good memories,
and leave the bad ones with me.
My heart is a padlocked tomb,
and I have thrown away the key…
I must go now.
Allow your memories of me to fade.

The ferryman awaits me,
and my ticket is paid.
So turn and walk away,
and don't ever look back.
Regrets are like a dead weights
around your neck.
They only serve to drag you down
into an abyss
of
Nothingness,
and
Non-existence.
Your persistence
is folly.
I am the Jolly Roger,
pirating the high seas
of
Purgatory.
The wind is at my back,
and I have hoisted my sails…
If all else fails,
I will allow the depths
of despair
to swallow me,
Until I have lost all feeling.
Until I yearn for nothing.
Until I am laid to rest…
We did our best,
but our best was never good enough.
The stuff of dreams
became the stuff of nightmares.
Life became a night terror
that flowed into day,

and just wouldn't go away…
"Have faith", they say.
But faith
to me
is a wraith,
that vanishes whenever I grasp at it…
Oblivion,
as black as obsidian
is my new religion,
and it is time to worship…
Amen.

Four Letter Word
By Sarah Dale

Love is a four letter word
More cursed than the secret name of god
That may not be spoken, or read,
May not be written or thought.

Staple your lips together,
Drive a nail through your tongue;
Redact the old texts
With a ruthless hand.

If you must write it
Replace each letter
With an asterisk
Making a string of stars.

When you have done
Seal it in a lead box;
Drown it deeper
Than the bones of whales.

Do not dare think it
Behind closed eyes;
Love is a filthy, dirty
Four letter word.

Ladder
By Sarah Dale

I'd take your advice
To get over it
But somehow
No matter where I look
I can't find a ladder
Long enough

I asked the tooth fairy
And the fire brigade
And the old woman
Who washes the moon's face
To lend me a ladder
Long enough

But they all said,
"We're sorry, but we use
Our ladders 24/7"
So I can't find a ladder
Long enough
To get over it

Lights
By Scarlett Ward

Maybe that's why I wanted to sit so close to you,
Because my eyes were greedy;
I wanted the light
Rebounding from your face
To enter my eyes first
Before anyone else's
So that I was the next thing
That it touched after you,
Without it being spoilt
by anyone else's second-hand reflection-
and that would somehow bring us closer,
perhaps it maintained small traces of you-
I squeeze my eyes shut
As though to keep the light trapped in my pupils-
As though pressing hard on the back of a stamp
To get a clearer impression.
I let each curl of your hair
And every freckle on your jaw
Sear into my memory
So that next time I leave
I have defined indentations in my mind of your
likeness
For times when I am much further away,
And I rely upon this light-burnt photograph
Developing in the darkroom of my brain
To recall every detail
That I am so greedy to remember.

Infrared
By Scarlett Ward

You were never designed to be
appreciated only by eyes
that cannot see further
than where light lends them its strength.

You are Braille for the feeling mind;
The streak of violet against black
when I press my palms into my eyelids.
Vision cheats you- for you are infrared;

There is so much of you
invisible to their naked eyes
but seen so clearly by mine.

I've stared at the sun too long
and come the twilight hours,
memories of burning shapes
dance on my eyelashes still,
Like sharp frost on dead branches.

From Darkness to Light
By Scott Cowley

Pulls on a new pair of kicks,
Looks in the mirror and tips himself a wink.
Pulls open the front door, unlocked.
Looks down at his watch less wrist,
Gives a wry smile at what he thinks,
The fact time means little to nothing.

With fight inside he strides,
The day's no longer dark as night.
With fight inside he strides,
With days he's turned from dark to light.

How he got here
That does matter.
He's been battered,
He's been beaten.
Face down with a crippling affliction,
With days as black as nights.

He strides,
Dark as night.
With fight,
Dark to light.

The fact of matter he's risen from beaten,
The fact of the matter shrugged off battered.
Even though his bones clattered,
Even though his mind was tattered.
Through gritted teeth stained chipped,
Striving forward determined yet haggard.

Waist deep through disconnected disassociation.
Through unjust decisions and justifications.
Breaking through from the outside,
Breaking through with head held high.

He strides,
Days no longer dark as night.

Crisis and Discovery
By Scott Cowley

Crisis and Recovery,
A journey of deep soul searching discovery.
Don't smother, don't cover me,
This is my time you'll get over me.

Lost in time all hovery.
Sat on cliff edge don't bother me.
Section 136 to try and smother me,
Here and now simplicity.

This name, this name you gave to me,
Who am I who am I to be?
Can't sleep for nights,
Smoke drink a brew with me.
Is this how it's supposed to be?

Step follows step,
Deliberate not expertly.
You've asked who,
Who gave these words to me?
You put a mic,
A Mic in front of me,
Is this how it ought to be.

You'll find peace,
Where your peace will be.
This is now
A time for me to be.
I'm no preacher,
No god to be.

This is;
My crisis
My recovery
My journey
My discovery.

Insatiable
By Sian Jansen-Bowen

When demons' arms caress your weak and flabby
shell,
They will shed you of your mortal skin and red
ribbons of flesh will rain down.
They will dance in the storm of your loss and relish
in the waves of your pain,
They are unafraid.
They are hungry.

You are a mere morsel of pleasure to be devoured
too quickly to even taste,
Unable to nourish them in this life,
A crowded echo on their saturated palettes.

So now you must strive to be all you can be, and
when consumed...
You must be divine and joyful in the knowledge
that you are seasoned to perfection,
Even if these creatures cannot savour the scraps of
your being
You will know that no other shared your flavour
and no other ever will.

Only what is lost will be remembered...
Once your sticky juices have been lapped from
fiendish fingers far too fast,
They will know: you were the finest meal to cross
their puckered lips.

Soon, realisation will stab into their tongues

Ever after rending them unfulfilled and bitter,
Stalked by appetite, left unsatisfied and hollow,
All turns to ash too charred and hard to swallow.

I am
By Sian Jansen-Bowen

I am the morning, bearing down
A dew dropped glistening golden crown
I filter softly through the drapes
Brown eyes spring open as she wakes
She sinks into the sheets and hides
Her arms pressed tightly to her sides
The cotton cave is safe and warm
But never keeps her from my storm

I am the day that she must face,
Without my beauty or my grace...
what is this day to one so blind?
She cannot seek, so will not find.
Every moment seems such a waste,
to one without a bud of taste.
My light is shielded from her eyes
By creeping fog and clouds of lies.

I am the evening, drifting past
I'm almost gone and fading fast
I linger only to reach out
One last attempt to scream and shout
"Don't give up, you brown-eyed flower
Not every day will be so sour
You are not yet all you can be
So don't you dare give up on me."

I am the night, a dark embrace
A welcome friend and resting place
This empty vessel cannot see

Everything she means to me
I wrap her softly in my arms
I kiss her nose, her lips, her palms
Her eyelids flicker up at me
At last a hopeful spark I see.

Family
By Simon Farrant

It started when I was eleven
'Me and your Mother don't love each other
anymore'
The end of being a child and opening a closed door
My parents were the first to separate in my class
The first of many more

As the years roll by
Time gets ever shorter
At first I tried my best to keep in touch
A one way street was always around the corner
Losing the last fourteen years
Hasn't made me any poorer

There are no regrets for me
I prefer to move forward in my life
Now there's my three kids
As well as my awesome wife

For her being a kid was tough
Not many smooth roads
Much more became rough
Our paths crossed one day
Two people with family history

We chose to be together in this life
Ten years we've been wed
For both of us our family is special
Times have been both bad and good

We have learned from the past years
That we don't need to fear
The future days
Because they are not yet here

Just take one day at a time
Look to the future days and years
Let's work hard to get there
Love plus happiness and the birthday bear

Santa hand in hand with the tooth fairy

They may well be legendary
Together we can break the ladders
Of generation past and bridges burned
Stay strong keep love keep true

Advocate Participate and laughter
This is Yours and Mine
Forever to treasure
We will succeed
And darkness of the past
Will retreat to be Old Days

Family Forever.

Now and Then
By Steve Harrison

Every now and again
The odd occasion
But never the second, fourth or sixth time
Never even stevens
On that odd occasion
All becomes clear
Unfamiliar fading faces look focussed and clear
Eyes piercing back through the fog
But usually
Now & then mix up
Past and present introduce themselves
Lost keys to forgotten doors
Objects lose their names
Nothing gets remembered no mirrors in their
blanked faces
Securely trapped in the present
A strange mindfulness
Then & now
Now & then

New Start
By Steve Harrison

Amongst the new leaves,
fresh sheets and clean slates wiped by cloths
 still wearing unwrapped creases
I give you a bottle of ink.
A blue glass lagoon to float your thoughts within
 left to Sun dry, evaporated salt flat
 sediment, soak in to paper, reader, observer.
Take care in search of stainless scripts
watch out for accidental finger prints.
Keep that mistaken blotter to hand.
Choose either Poundland pens,
 ceramic ink wells with steel point nibs
 or a brass levered Bakelite pen.
 Pump the blue life blood,
fill the rubber sack with careful strokes.
 Let it all flow with saturated thoughts
 soaking just one side of the paper.
Wear away the nibs with well-chosen words,
 sentences that skip across the page
and don't look back.
Treat the world to your thoughts,
to notes in cards, stonking stories,
new novellas, flashier fiction.
 Fill other people's mouths with your scripts.

You can be the wordsmith's match.
Ignite me
Illuminate the world.

The Prisoner
By Steve C. Davis

Sunlight streaming
Through high window in tower.
Sunlight on faded stones
And worn bricks.
And far below
The prisoner watches.

You Stand in the Dark
By Steven C. Davis

You stand in the dark, watching them breathe.
Afraid to look,
and the waves wash upon the shore
and the tide turns.
And the moment is gone, and you turn.
And then silence,
and the water waits by the reef
out of reach,
and you're falling out of the sky,
as the ground rises.
Then in silence, your new born star,
draws breath once again,
and the ground gives way to the sky
as feathers flutter by.
He lies on his back, a smile adorned,
not knowing why.
You stand in the dark, watching him breathe,
afraid to look,
and the waves wash upon the shore,
and the tide.

Light
By Sunayna Pal

Dark scary rain
slowly reducing to gray.
Loud thunderous clouds
starting to part away
The bright yellow shine,
swiftly making its way

All is not well yet
but will be.
Beautiful rainbow
stands in glory
Thus we turn a page
of this long story.

Glimpse
By Tina Cole

I took down the mirrors last winter
to keep you out of sight,

turned down the lights
to keep shadows on best behaviour

& hid the sun in a low place.
In High Street windows

I caught a glimpse among the deceit
of wonky mannequins

where the clouded eye
high in the marbled shopping mall

was always green winking vigilant.
Were you caught in that speed trap flash

while the shadows in the rear view mirror
kept up their zealous stalking?

Tonight a framed stare is reflected back
in the jittery flickerings of the late news

like a black and ragged bird
seeking something shiny

Elsewhere
By Tina Cole

It was not I
yet inside this nightmare
I try to be elsewhere,
seek out quiet places,
stare in silence
where scenery is not evocative
or provocative,
in a mild season
late Autumn maybe
when the tear of sky is full of falling.

 I try to sleep
but prickles of memory stick
me to this sharp dark
filled with images I cannot un-scream.
I want to hide, avoid this shame
a long freight train moan
of knowledge that cannot be
un-known. It was not I
who left her all alone.

I try to conjure her.
Actualise days full of childish
chatter but the clatter of memory
is like broken plates & rage
like bees in an empty can,
another day stealing
breath away and no space
for me under all this waste
of sky.

I know Summer's tricks
are done, so, revert
seek a sun lost in Winter thickets
walk tense fields
far from home
where thick brambles
wait their chance to scar.

Stare, think of elsewhere.

The Last Prayer
By Tina Negus

He was the last man on earth, who prayed,
though since he rarely spoke of it, he assumed
there were others like him.

He had tried explaining it once,
to a girl he had thought he loved, but she laughed,
did not understand its importance to him.

It's not God in the sky, he tried, not an old bloke
with a long white beard, surrounded by cherubs
and seraphs... though it might be, he reflected.

But surely, she had replied, it is all about genetics
and psychology, astrophysics and biochemistry,
and he had given up on his attempt and merely
stated

it's what makes these things you mention tick,
it is the cause of light and life and has no quarrel
with the physical forces that you list.

It is, he said, with complete conviction, what keeps
the universe in existence, though he still had no
notion
that he was the last, the last man on earth who
prayed.

But it turned out he **was** the last, and he was right,
against all likely odds, for when he died
the universe imploded.

Gravestone
By Tina Negus

We are halted in our churchyard perambulation
by the gravestone, like wandering elephants,
finding
the bones of one of their own on the savannah
pathway.
The inscription sharpens and fades; the slanting
light
comes and goes as clouds
scud across the equinoctial sky.
briefly darkening the noon sun.
It is our great, great, great, great, great Grandfather
buried here, Thomas born 1756.

We walk around the plot, as elephants solemnly
circle
the thigh bone of an ancestor, aware somehow of
relationship:
this one is ours.
The adjacent memorial is to his daughter, Jane,
married
to the local publican; a third is no doubt ours too,
though
erosion over two centuries of the ornate limestone
slab
is too much for legibility, maybe?
it is for Thomas' first wife, Ann, who died
childless..
leaving his second wife Mary to produce ten
children
in eleven years.

We touch the stone, stroking its
roughness, like elephants
querying the gleaming skull with
their exploring trunks.
Our fingers trace the date of death, the carved pious
sentiment,
as elephants questioning the identity of the African
skeleton,
acknowledging their affinity, recognising the
belonging bones.

We have no family here to share our find, unlike the
elephants,
who nudge their young towards whitened rib and
jaw,
as though displaying a portrait of granny from the
photograph album,
yet we draw close together in common feeling, as
the elephants
lean in to each other and entwine their trunks
in familiar comfort.

Eventually, having deciphered as much of
the weathered runes
as we are able, we give the gravestone a final pat,
a backward glance when we leave, just like
the elephants…

Sanctuary
By Vicki MacWinyers

Back & forth the waves roll in
Challenging the beach
The foaming surf offers up a dream
That so far is out of reach

I wish I could live among the waves
Like the seal that I've just seen
Without a care for what comes next
Or for what has ever been

To swim among gigantic whales
Majestic in their song
Content with life - to carry on
Knowing they belong

To fly up high above the swell
Like the seagulls do
Playing in the clouds of spray
They all know the truth

Happiness is a gift

That we cannot take for granted
In the profoundness of the ocean
Seeds of hope will now be planted

Back & forth the waves roll in
Their cycle never ends
My life continues to evolve
The sea will help me mend.

Contemplation
By Vicki MacWinyers

I sit on a bench
On a hill
In the rain
Hiding my tears
My heart
Full of pain
I watch
I listen
I wait in vain
For the answer
To a question
I can't explain

I sit on a bench
In a park
Full of history
Surrounded by people
Who pass by
But can't see me
I am hurt
I am broken
And they let me be
A girl
On a bench
Across from the abbey

I sit on my bench
In quiet
Contemplation
A man walks by

On his face
Admiration
He smiles
He sees
The hurt and frustration
Of the girl
On the bench
Who has no conviction

He sits on my bench
On the hill
In the rain
He asks me
To share my fear
And my pain
I speak
He listens
And I smile again
On a bench
With a friend
On a hill in the rain

Thank you to……

Every amazing poet soul who has contributed their fantastic work for such a great cause.

The wonderful people who have encouraged me throughout the compilation and publication of this book. I am honoured and humbled.

Everyone who has purchased a copy of this book. Even if you don't like it, you've made a contribution to a fantastic charity.

Mind. My mind, your mind, any mind ignoring the limelight. We know who you are and we salute you. Enjoy and please put it to good use.

Becky Narron for the cover artwork.

My Family.

Helen, my Wife. Without you I am nothing and none of this would have been possible!

pAul

Printed in Great Britain
by Amazon